GW00725967

GOLDEN
RETRIEVERS

GOLDEN RETRIEVERS

JANE McDONALD

Photographs by Isabelle Français

Ariel Books

Andrews and McMeel

Kansas City

ISBN: 0-8362-2110-9

Library of Congress Catalog Card Number: 96-83361

CONTENTS

INTRODUCTION

Brains blend with beauty in golden retrievers. These versatile dogs, affectionately called "goldens," are revered as devoted family pets, elegant show dogs, expert trackers and game retrievers, and guide dogs for the blind. Once you begin to get to know your golden, his keen intelligence, undying devotion, and gentle playfulness will endear him quickly to you. You'll soon see why golden retrievers are very special dogs indeed.

The story of Poudre illustrates one golden's loyalty, stamina, and heroism. Poudre's owner Dale named his golden retriever after the nearby Poudre River, where he liked to go fly-fishing. It had rained for a few days, but this warm September morning dawned sunny and clear, so Poudre and Dale jumped in his truck and headed to the river.

As Dale started down the embankment toward the river, his feet slipped on the wet rocks, and he tumbled the rest of the way. The next thing he

knew he was lying face up in the water with his head wedged between two rocks, his right arm shattered, and his dog by his side. Dazed and disoriented, Dale was barely conscious, but he knew that Poudre was his only hope.

He grabbed her collar with his left hand, and told her to pull him. Poudre pulled and strained her 100-pound frame until she had gotten her 180-pound master to the riverbank. But Dale was so weak he couldn't even stand up, much less climb up the steep riverbank to the truck.

Once again, he grabbed Poudre's

collar, and she dragged him slowly but surely over the rough rocks and up the sheer embankment. Although exhausted by the effort, she did not stop until they reached Dale's truck. Dale lost a lot of fishing equipment to the river that day, but thanks to Poudre, he didn't lose his life.

Few people will experience such a dramatic rescue by a golden retriever, but golden owners recommend them as the ideal all-around family dog. Easy to own and easy to care for, they are renowned for their natural love of people, especially of children, and for their physical beauty and delightful temperament.

YOUR GOLDEN RETRIEVER

HISTORY OF
THE BREED

The true origins of the golden retriever were shrouded in mystery until the second half of this century. For many years the story had circulated that this regal breed was descended from a rather unlikely source: a troupe of Russian circus dogs that were performing in Brighton, England, in 1858.

Legend had it that Sir Dudley Marjoribanks, the first Lord Tweedmouth, was so impressed by the intelligence, cleverness, and unusual pale yellow color of these Russian dogs that he purchased the entire team and took them back to his estate in Scotland, where he trained them to hunt deer. It was said that all goldens were descended from this well-traveled and talented troupe.

However delightful this tale may be, it was disproved in 1952 by Lord Tweedmouth's great-nephew, the sixth

Earl of Ilchester. The earl methodically researched Lord Tweedmouth's kennel logs and found no mention of the exotic Russian circus dogs. He did, however, discover a more believable story that has since been accepted as the real history of the golden retriever breed.

According to his great-nephew's research, in 1865 Lord Tweedmouth purchased one "yellow retriever" from a Brighton cobbler, who had accepted the dog as payment for a debt. This dog was the sole yellow puppy in an unregistered litter of black wavy-coated retrievers. Lord Tweedmouth named him "Nous."

For over twenty years, Lord Tweedmouth carefully pursued his goal of breeding a high-quality, hunting and game retrieval dog from his first yellow retriever, Nous. We owe the color, build, temperament, intelligence, and tracking abilities of today's goldens to his meticulous breeding strategy.

Lord Tweedmouth bred Nous with a Tweed Water spaniel named Belle, and a litter of four bitches resulted. They were bucolically named: Ada, Primrose, Crocus, and Cowslip; these retriever-cross-spaniel dogs are the true ancestors of all golden retrievers.

Over the years, Lord Tweedmouth crossed the evolving goldens, often called "yellows" at the time, with other sporting dog breeds in order to add distinct characteristics to the line. More Tweed Water spaniels (bred for flushing game) supplied stamina, swimming ability, and a pleasant temperament; an Irish setter (bred for pointing birds) contributed agility in hilly terrain and a dash of color; wavy-coated retrievers provided hunting ability and intense retrieving desire; and a sandy-colored bloodhound improved the scenting and tracking ability of the breed.

In 1903 the Kennel Club of England accepted the first golden retrievers for registration. In 1911 the Golden Retriever Club of England was formed. Serious breeding of golden retrievers did not occur in the United States until 1932, when they were first officially recognized

by the American Kennel Club. At that time, they were still considered a rare breed; from 1932 to 1956, only 20,376 goldens were regis-

tered. Today, however, golden retrievers rank among the four most popular breeds in the United States; over 64,300 were registered in 1994 alone.

PHYSICAL
CHARACTERISTICS

Probably the first thing you'll notice in a golden is his regal head and friendly and intelligent expression. His twinkling eyes should be almost almond-shaped; his feathery ears should fall close to his cheeks. Typically, a slight smile seems to play around his mouth, contributing to an overall impression of congeniality.

Retrievers are tremendously curious about their environment. Like all dogs, they are able to move each ear independently, to scan their surroundings carefully with their keen sense of hearing. Dogs see in black and white, and their range of vision is wider than that of humans. Your golden also has more light

receptors in his eyes than you do, so when it's twilight for you, he still sees relatively clearly, as if it were still afternoon.

Golden retrievers' physical beauty, trainability, and elegant bearing make them superb show dogs. As for all other registered breeds, the American Kennel Club has established a "breed standard" for golden retrievers. The standard is a detailed written description outlining ideal physical traits of the head, eyes, teeth, nose, ears, neck, forequarters, hindquarters, feet, tail, coat, color, gait, movement, general appearance, and size.

Of course, there is really no such thing as the "perfect" dog, but the standard serves as an ideal toward which all serious breeders strive, and is the basis for dog show judges' decisions. The standard also ensures the continued purity and health of the breed.

The typical golden retriever has a thick, silky coat that ranges in color from cream to dark gold, and is longer on his neck, tail, and the backs of his legs. White in the coat is undesirable, although a few white hairs on the chest will not disqualify a dog from competition. Golden retrievers are generally slimmer and lankier in build than Labrador retrievers. The standard for goldens calls for adult male dogs to measure between 23–24 inches from ground to shoulders, and weigh 65–75 pounds, whereas the slightly smaller females should measure between $21\frac{1}{2}$ and $22\frac{1}{2}$ inches and

weigh between 55–65 pounds.

A golden's body is muscular and well-balanced. Romping in the fields or trotting through the woods, a golden retriever moves at a smooth and powerful gait. Thanks to superb coordination and balance, his movement appears almost effortless. This muscular efficiency is also what allows him to run or hunt for long periods without total exhaustion. You could play outdoors all day with your golden, and he would probably just hanker for more!

BEHAVIORAL CHARACTERISTICS

By nature, goldens are gentle, friendly, and fun-loving. Their overwhelming desire to please

makes them a perfect household pet. You may at first have to restrain a golden's natural exuberance with very young children or the elderly, but once your dog understands the house rules, he will be more than happy to abide by them. You also will need to learn to respect your golden's particular personality and way of demonstrating affection. Some love to be hugged and cuddled, while others prefer to sit, contented and proud at your feet.

There is one drawback to goldens' legendary friendliness: they do not shine as guard dogs. They will warn you of approaching strangers, but most goldens see strangers as potential playmates!

Goldens are not particularly suited to apartment living, but they will adapt to living in your house. It is important to remember that they were carefully bred as hunting dogs. They love to romp

and run outdoors, and indeed their general well-being depends on frequent sportive sorties. If you don't live in the country, find a park nearby so your golden can exercise correctly. He needs these rambunctious excursions for his health and happiness.

The Great Outdoors calls more

loudly to golden retrievers than to many other dog breeds. Their intelligence and trainability complement their physical superiority to make them ideal hunting partners. Most goldens are natural retrievers and will instinctively pick up anything thrown their way. They are easily trained, and they have acute scenting and tracking abilities. They also love swimming, and their dense, water-repellent coat allows them to dive into the iciest waters to retrieve game. Remarkably, a well-trained golden can retrieve waterfowl and other game in his soft mouth without even bruising it!

YOUR GOLDEN RETRIEVER PUPPY

CHOOSING A PUPPY

Choosing a golden retriever puppy will be a difficult task when you are faced with an entire litter of cute pups racing to greet you with tails wagging! To make an intelligent and ultimately satisfying choice, some research and forethought are essential. Luckily, both male and female golden retrievers possess gracious temperaments and are easy to live with. So the choice of your golden's gender is a purely personal one for you to make.

First, learn everything you can about golden retrievers; talk to other golden owners, local breeders, or your local veterinarian. The time you spend

now looking for just the right puppy will pay off many times over in the future, so be patient.

Next, make appointments with a few golden retriever kennels in your area. Pet stores are a less reliable source; they may not have golden puppies when you wish to buy one, and they also have much less invested than the breeder does in the past pedigree and future well-being of their little charges. Breeders take great pride in their dogs and in their kennels' reputations, and take great care to maintain both.

In any case, you are looking for

an alert, happy, and well-bred puppy. When you arrive at the breeder's, make sure the premises look and smell clean, and that the puppies greet you eagerly and playfully. Goldens are "people" dogs; their innate friendliness should be apparent even at a young age.

Physically, look for golden puppies who are plump, sturdy, and healthy. All puppies have some "baby fat"

that gives them an endearing puppy paunch, but a noticeably distended stomach could indicate the presence of worms. Also check that the puppy's eyes and nose are free of discharge, and that his eye-rims, nose, and lips are jet-black, a sign of good pigmentation as well as good health. The color of a puppy's coat always darkens as he matures, but the color of his ears will usually closely resemble his eventual adult coloring.

Before you leave the kennel, the breeder should give you a written record of all shots and wormings the puppy has received, as well as precise feeding instructions.

PUPPY CARE

In all the excitement of choosing a puppy, it's easy to forget about the practical supplies you

will need for this important new addition to your household. Here are a few essentials you should buy before you pick up your pup: two large weighted bowls for food and water; a pin brush and canine nail cutters for grooming your golden; a combination leash and adjustable collar, called a "show lead"; and a wire crate or cage measuring about twenty-two inches wide by twenty-six inches high by thirty-two inches long, which will be your golden's bedroom, dining room, and personal sanctuary during his first year.

A few words about the crate: at first, the idea of a wire crate may not sound particularly appealing to you, but rest assured that there is absolutely noth-ing cruel or uncomfortable about it for the dog. On the contrary, dogs are den

animals; they feel safest, happiest, and most comfortable in confined spaces. At first, your puppy should spend time in his

crate when you cannot properly supervise him. And this crate will also be invaluable when you housebreak your puppy, and when he's teething.

When the big day arrives to pick up your new family member from the breeder, line the floor of the crate with thick newspapers, and take the crate along so the puppy can ride home in his new "house."

When he arrives in your home, your puppy may at first be unhappy, confused, and disoriented. Remember, this entire experience is quite traumatic and bewildering for any golden at such a tender age. After you have put him back in his crate for his first night in your home, you might want to place a ticking alarm clock or a hot water bottle wrapped in a towel in with him; these items reas-

sure the puppy by reminding him of his mother.

Your puppy's first night might be difficult for you too! Many golden pups will whimper and cry in their crate, but golden experts agree that you should never give in and take him out of his crate the first few nights. Your golden's loneliness will pass in a day or two, and he'll soon settle happily into your family's routines.

Goldens are "mouthy" dogs and enjoy a good chew at any age, so buy your puppy some toys such as hard nylon bones or hard rubber balls. He will start teething at about four months, and not only are these toys good for the puppy's oral health, but it's certainly better for him to gnaw on a rawhide chew toy than on an electric cord or your brand-new shoes.

A day or two after you bring your golden home, take him to your veterinarian for a checkup and for any necessary shots. Consult the breeder's inoculation information to see whether the puppy has had shots against distemper, hepatitis, leptospirosis, rabies, parvovirus, and parainfluenza. This first visit is an important time to establish a good relationship with your vet; he will be your golden's trusted doctor for many years to come.

BONDING

The period between three to twelve weeks of age is crucial to a puppy's development. The first couple of weeks are devoted to canine socialization, as the puppy learns valuable lessons from his mother and his littermates in how dogs should behave. During the next several weeks (somewhere between five and twelve weeks of age), the puppy will be ready to form permanent bonds to his pack or to his family, and this is the best period—

ideally in the eighth week—for the puppy to move into his new home.

A careful breeder or owner will already have accustomed puppies to gentle handling early on. As a new owner, you should try to minimize stress on your puppy, paying close attention, handling and talking to him frequently, introducing him to all the members of his new family, both human and animal (under supervision and preferably one at a time), and providing him with a safe, but not an isolated, place to rest.

Goldens are social animals and yours will crave attention and frequent play dates from you. Early training and rambunctious exercise outings will also help you get to know your puppy's unique personality and to establish a deep and lasting bond with him. As with any new friend, it takes care, time, curiosity, and

understanding to discover all the delights of his character.

You'll soon look at your growing golden retriever with heartfelt appreciation for the joy he brings to your life, and see him as a welcome companion on all occasions.

BASIC TRAINING

Feeding and housebreaking your golden are the first tasks to tackle. Follow the breeder's feeding instructions to the letter; at this point, your puppy's digestion is fragile and you don't want to upset his stomach.

Until he is about three months old, you should feed your golden three or four times a day in his personal dining room, his crate. Puppies also need to have fresh water available, but place the water dish outside of the crate, since many playful puppies mistake it for an opportunity to take a refreshing swim! As your puppy matures, he will eat larger portions less frequently: from three to six months, decrease his feedings to three times a day; then from six months to one year, to twice a day.

Your little puppy has a lot to learn, and it is your responsibility as his owner to teach him the rules kindly but firmly. For example, begin house-training him immediately upon his arrival. Here, his crate plays a starring role; once the pup has claimed the crate as his "house," he will instinctively want to keep this space clean, and will make valiant efforts not to mess in it. With consistent and reliable help from you, he will quickly learn to "hold it" until he's outside his crate.

The house-training technique is simple. Establish a regular schedule of taking the puppy directly from his crate outdoors so he can relieve himself at least five times a day: first thing in the morning (before your shower or coffee), before you leave for the day, around noon, at dinner time, and lastly, just before bedtime. Wait until he does his duty before bringing him back inside your house. And of course, enthusiastic praise of your pup at these crucial moments outdoors will help the house-training process along.

When he does make a mistake indoors, reprimand him firmly by saying "No!"; *never* hit a puppy. As with a

human baby, try to be patient, tolerant, and understanding of your golden puppy's mistakes.

You also may start teaching your smart little fellow to come when called, to sit and stand on command, and to walk on a leash. Keep your commands simple, and be patient but firm.

Your golden retriever's first birthday is his rite of passage into adulthood. This is when his true beauty and delightful temperament will begin to shine. His puppy antics are over and you'll probably find that caring for your adult golden is a breeze!

Your Adult Golden Retriever

FOOD

You can expect an adult golden to eat between fifteen and twenty-five pounds of dry food per week, depending on his weight. He will need just one meal a day, and feeding him in the evening should help the dog sleep.

Like all active, outdoorsy dogs,

golden retrievers require proper nutrition to maintain their muscles and bones in excellent condition. Canned food and semimoist packets, which have a higher fat content and can lead to weight gain, should not account for more than a quarter of his food intake. The breeder or your local vet can suggest the best brands of commercial dog food to buy to ensure your dog's complete nutrition, and oral and digestive health.

Some owners supplement their dog's diet with table scraps—though you should never feed your dog directly from the table. A heavy beef knucklebone or marrowbone to chew on is a good idea, though you should parboil it to kill bacteria, and your dog should not actually eat the bone. Fish, chicken, or chop bones are strictly forbidden; they splinter easily and can seriously damage your dog's alimentary tract. Rawhide chews are a good substitute for bones.

TRAINING AND EXERCISE

Golden retrievers may benefit from training by a professional trainer as well as by the owner. Whether they conduct formal training themselves or not, owners need to participate with their dogs in a variety of activities. A golden loves nothing better than a good, rousing romp outside with his best friend, you. Regular, daily exercise is key for his health and

happiness, so try to arrange his exercise schedule with the following tips in mind.

Hard exercise should never immediately follow a meal; your golden needs a chance to let his food settle and to eliminate it before strenuously exerting himself. By the same token, after hard exercise, do not give your golden a great deal of water until he has had time to rest. A few slurps of water or a tidbit of food are fine; just don't overdo it.

Goldens are so companionable that they would much prefer to play with you than to play alone. If you let your golden outside expecting him to entertain himself, you might be sorely disappointed. Instead, he will probably gambol around a bit, then wait politely for you to join him. For variety, nylon dog Frisbee disks and balls are enjoyable and long-lasting toys for playing rollicking games of fetch or catch together.

GROOMING

Luckily, golden retrievers are naturally handsome and require little grooming to look their best. Thirty minutes of care every two weeks will keep your golden healthy and in top form.

While brushing your golden's coat, keep an eye out for fleas and ticks. Not only are they hazardous to the dog's health, but you certainly don't want them as permanent guests in your home. Should you find any, have your furry friend dusted, sprayed, or dipped immediately.

Lift up his soft ears to make sure that they are clean inside. If not, gently cleanse them with a solution recommended by your vet. Using canine nail

clippers, carefully trim the nailtips; keep in mind that trimming too close to the quick will hurt your golden retriever.

HEALTH

Goldens are generally hardy and healthy dogs, but there are several common canine problems to be aware of. Your golden may be somewhat prone to a wet eczema skin problem, called "hot spots," especially in the summer. And unfortunately, external parasites such as fleas, ear mites, and ticks may take up residence in your golden's lustrous coat. Your vet carries medical products to treat these problems quickly and easily. Remember also that your adult golden needs yearly testing for heartworm, and annual booster shots against the infectious canine diseases.

At the age of twelve to fifteen months, your golden retriever should be x-rayed for signs of hip dysplasia, a genetically inherited bone malformation affecting the hip sockets, especially of large breeds. There is no cure for this potentially crippling condition, so if it is detected you should not risk passing on the condition by breeding your dog.

Additionally, if you chose your dog primarily as a family pet, you should strongly consider neutering your male golden or spaying your female. It's a

simple veterinary procedure that will have no negative effect whatsoever on the dog; indeed, it will probably lengthen his or her life. In addition, neutered males and spayed females make better pets since they'll expend less energy in a starry-eyed search for a mate.

Showing and judging the conformation of dogs is considered a sport: the dog sport. Each year in the United States there are over ten thousand competitive events—dog shows, field trials, obedience trials. Each of the AKC-registered breeds has a national parent club that helps sponsor and organize licensed shows of various kinds.

The dog show, which emphasizes conformation, or how close competitors come to achieving the breed standard, is the most common kind of show. Categories for entry in a given show can include Puppy (sometimes divided into two separate age classes of six to nine months and nine to twelve months), Novice, Bred-by-Exhibitor, American-Bred, and Open. At licensed events, competitors win points toward titles. Overall winners of shows sponsored by individual breed clubs earn the title Best of Breed, and all-breed clubs sponsor shows leading to the title of Best in Show.

Five points is the maximum a competitor can win in one show; a dog that has won fifteen points in AKC-licensed shows is an AKC champion.

The best known and most prestigious dog show in the United States is

the annual event put on by the Westminster Kennel Club in New York. Every dog that enters Westminster is already a champion, and some exhibitors enter the competition simply for the honor of saying that their dogs participated in the Westminster show; the annual show book is a cherished keepsake.

The responsibility of a judge is heavy, and judges themselves are subject to strict requirements before they are accredited by the AKC. A judge is expected to have had at least ten years' dog-show experience before applying to be certified, must specify which breed (or breeds) he or she wishes to evaluate, must have owned or exhibited dogs of that breed, and must have bred at least four litters of the same breed. Furthermore, a candidate must have had five AKC stewarding assignments, pass a rules test and a test on breed standards, and supply references, in order to be accredited.

It is the judges who determine the winners of a show, but a judge can only make a decision about the best dog in any category on the basis of the field of competitors at that single event and on that single day. The knowledge that on a

different day, and in a different field of competitors, the judgments might well be very different, is part of the essence of the dog sport, a source of its fascination and its drama.

The text of this book was set in
Futura Book, with Odeon
Condensed display type.

Book design by Jaye Zimet